Tattoo Designs Realistic Birds

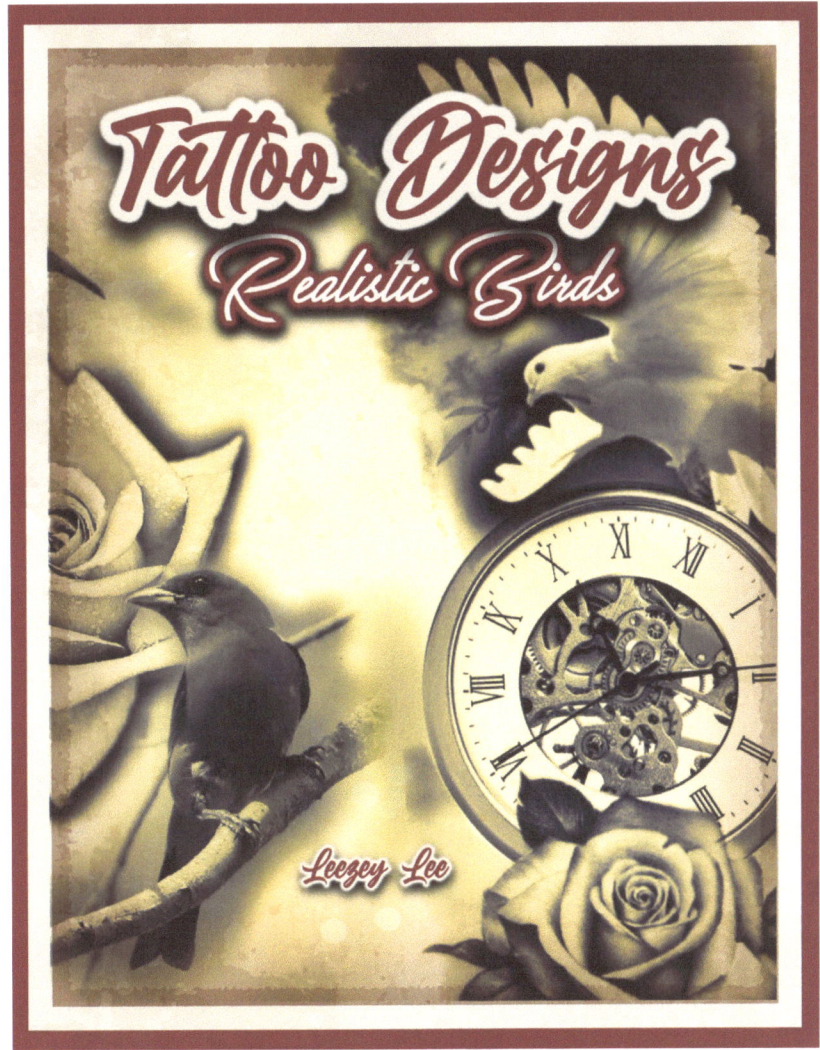

Leezey Lee

Tattoo Designs Realistic Birds
Leezey Lee
Copyright © 2021 Leezey Lee
All Rights Reserved.
ISBN: 9798475355121

Contents

1. Intro
2. Tattoos
3. About Autor

Intro

welcome

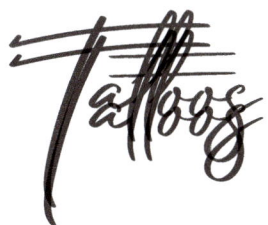

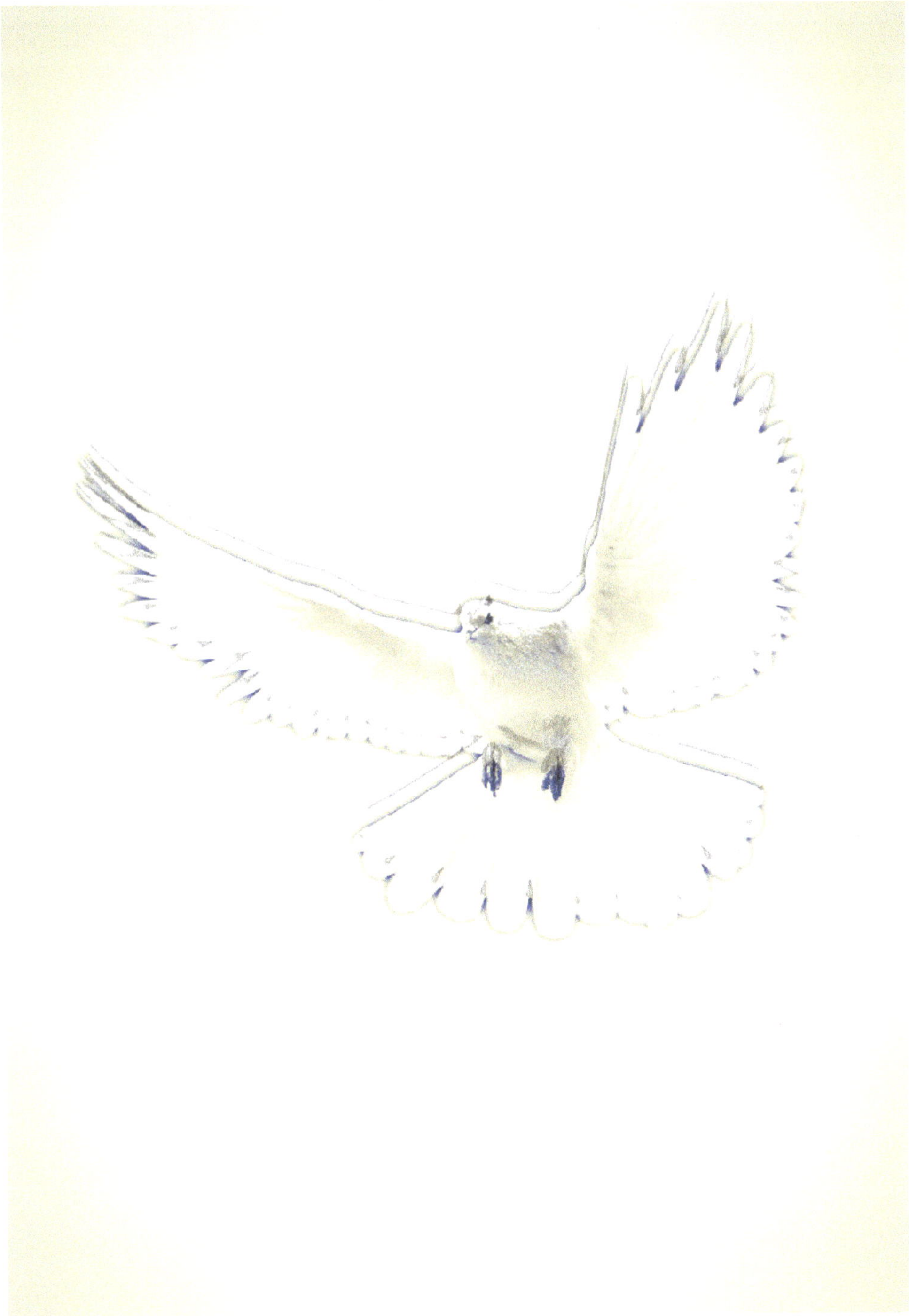

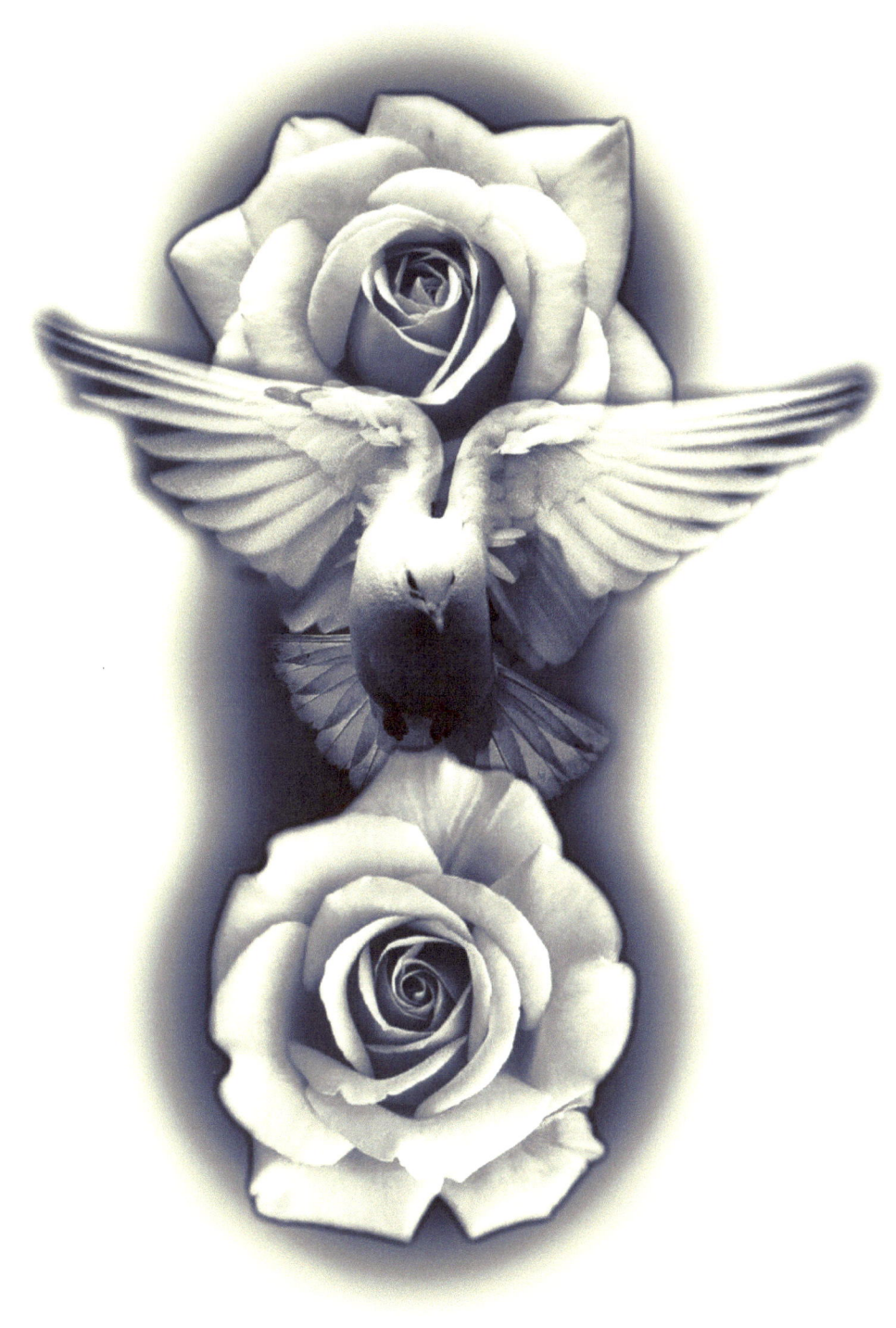

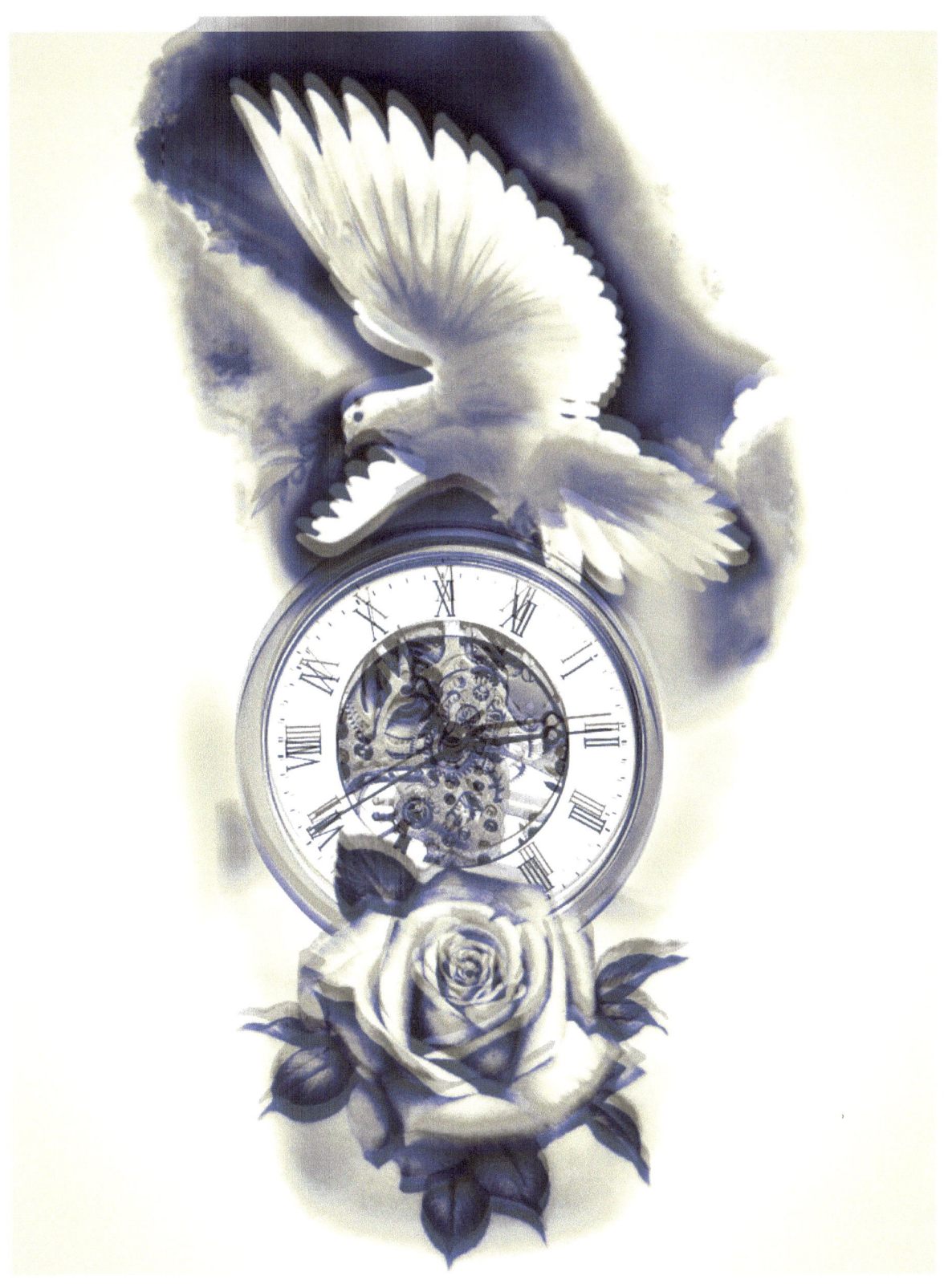

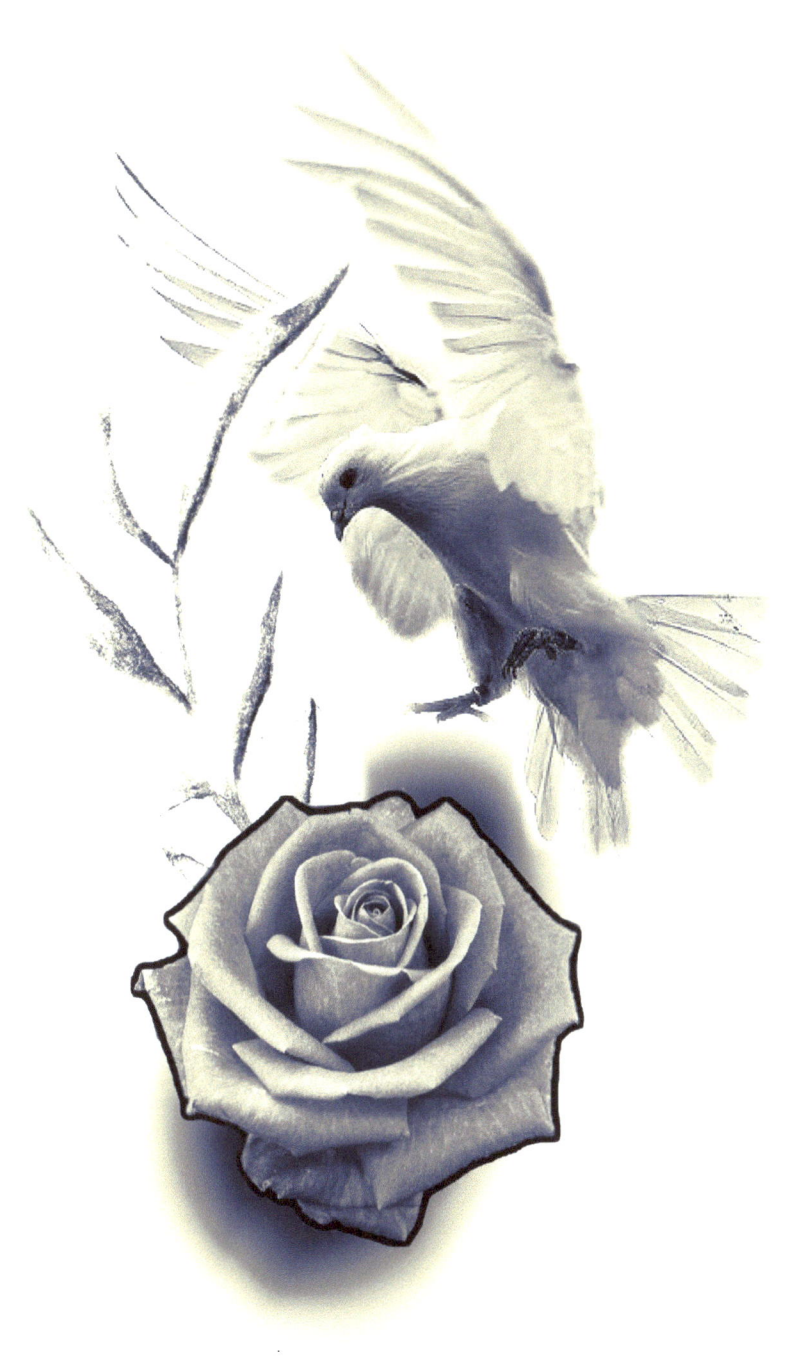

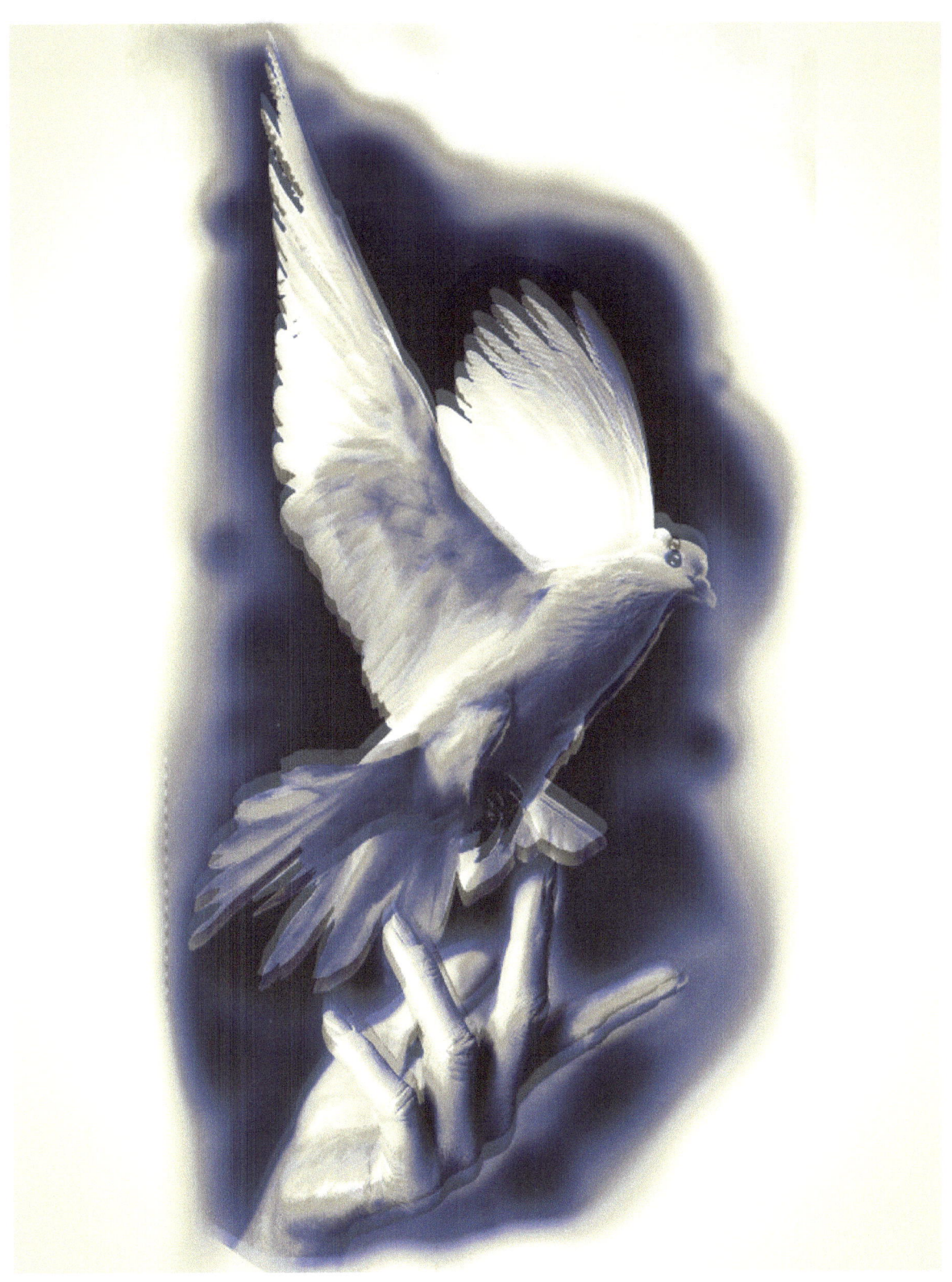

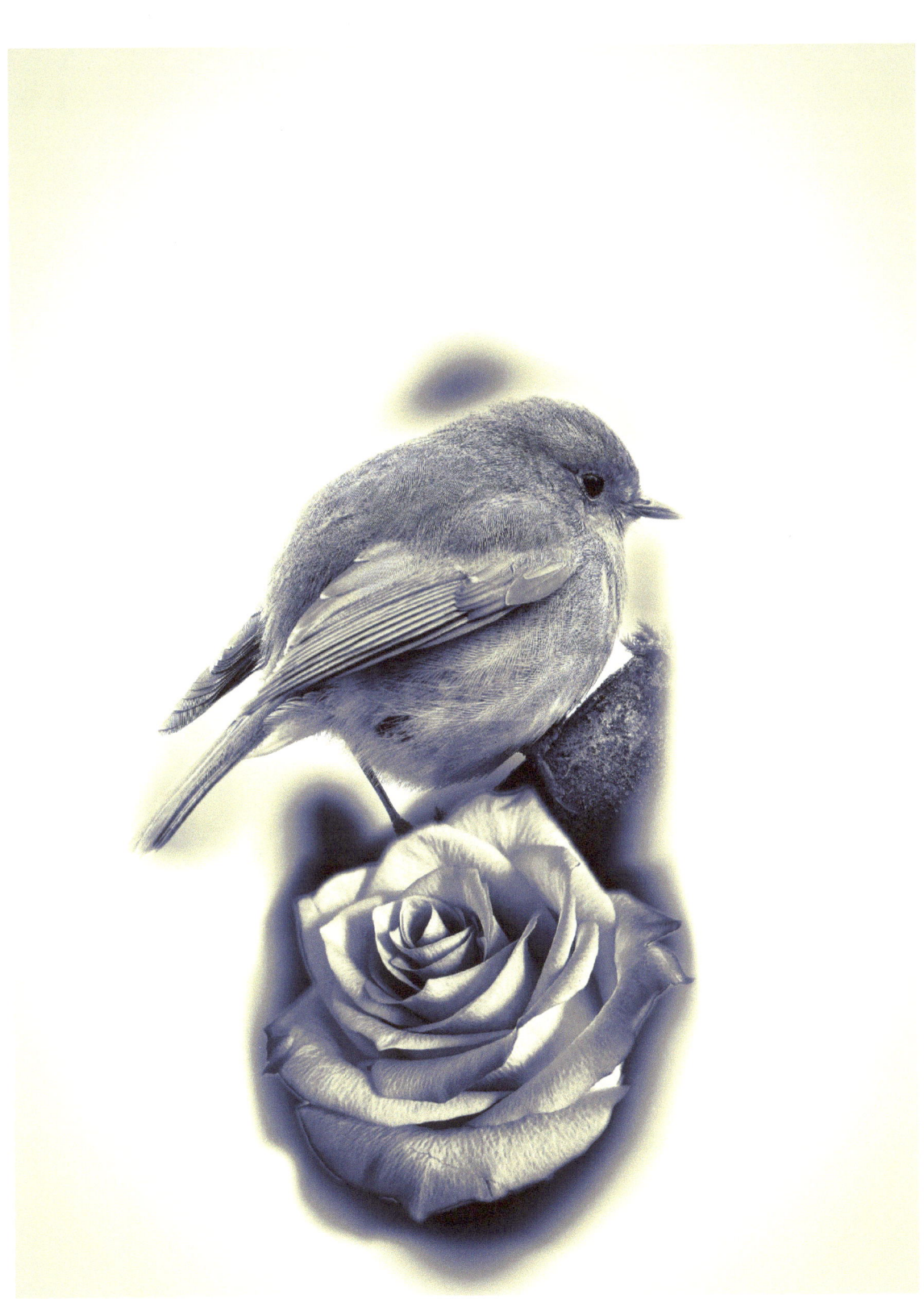

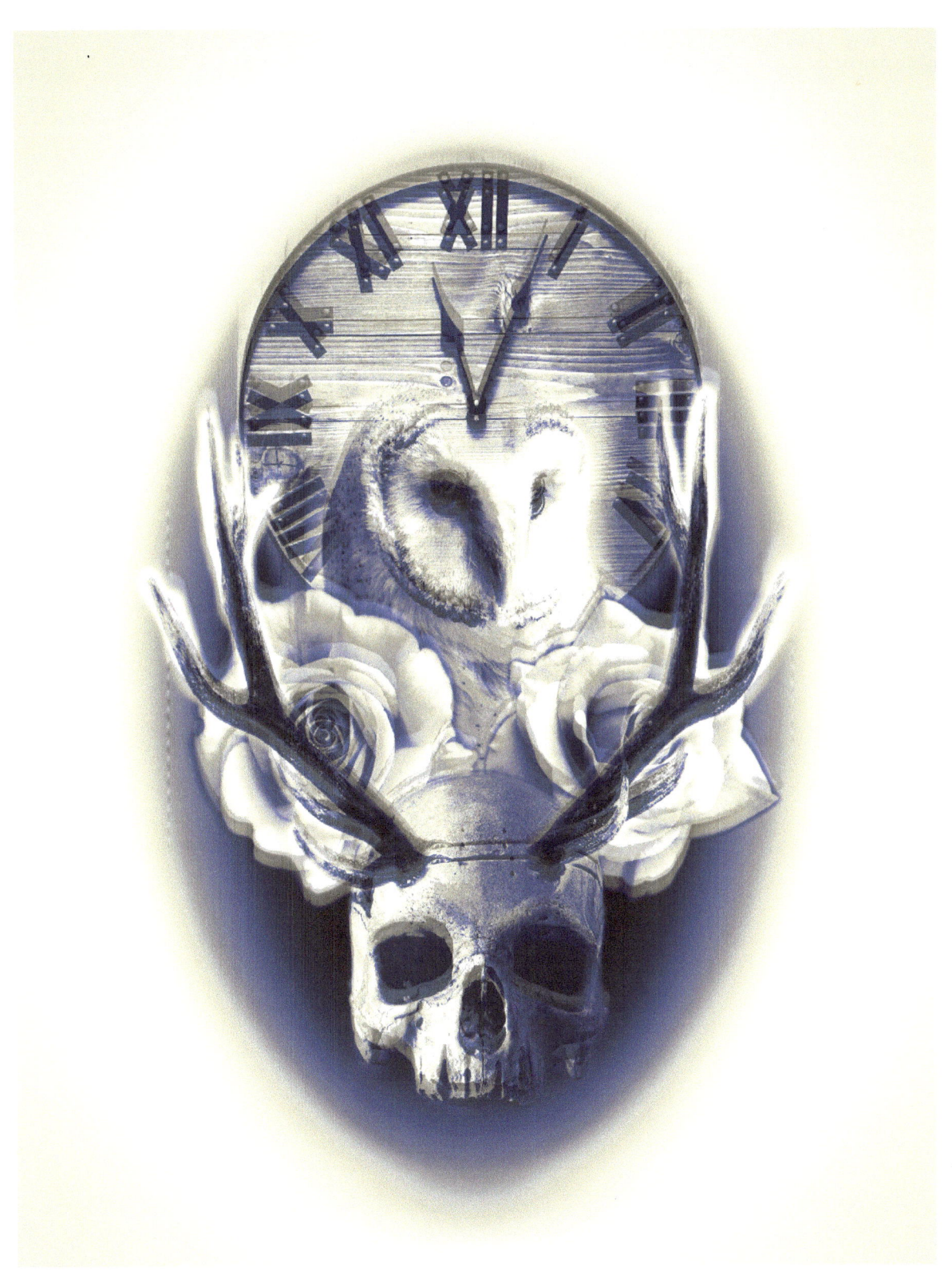

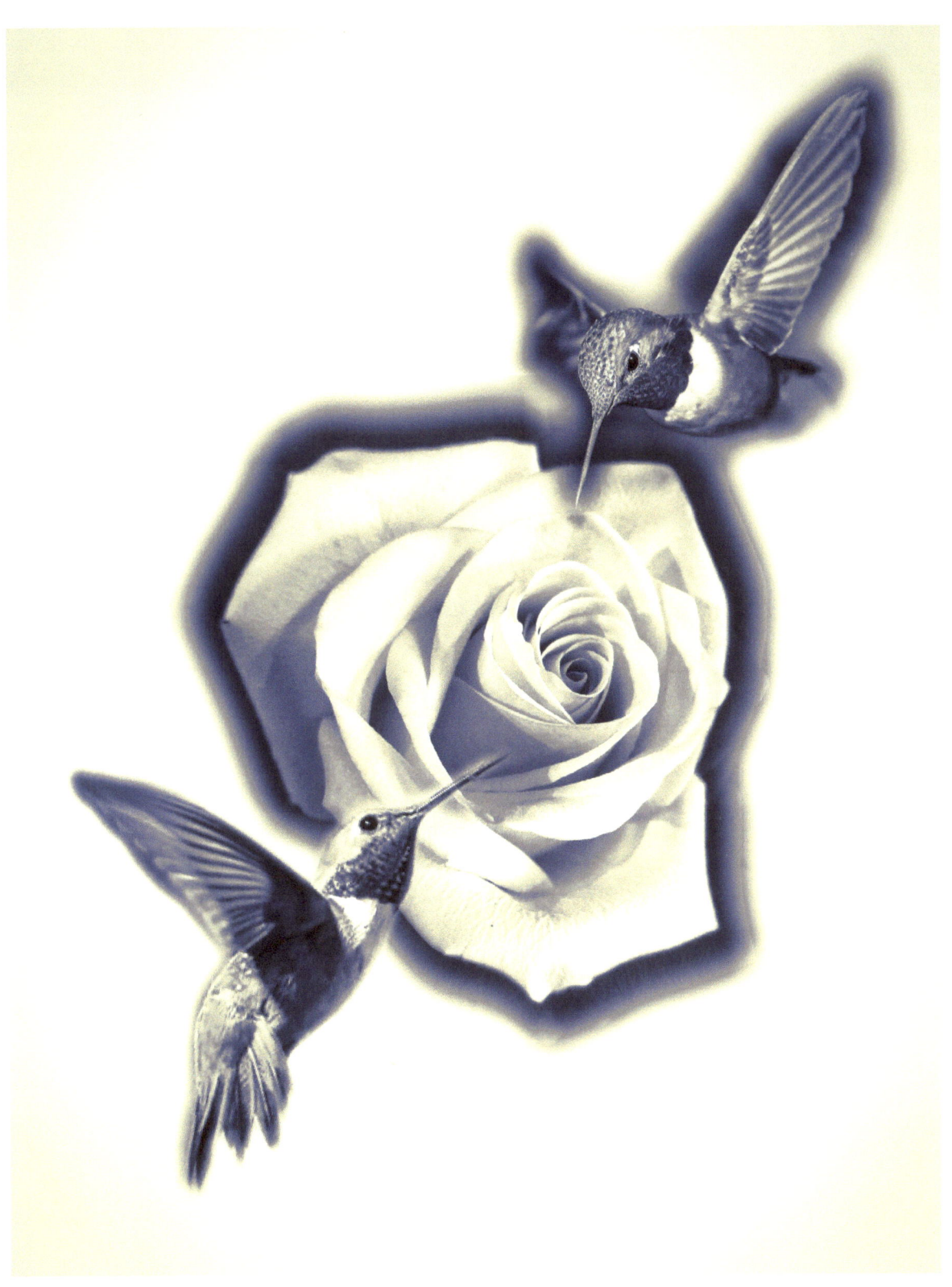

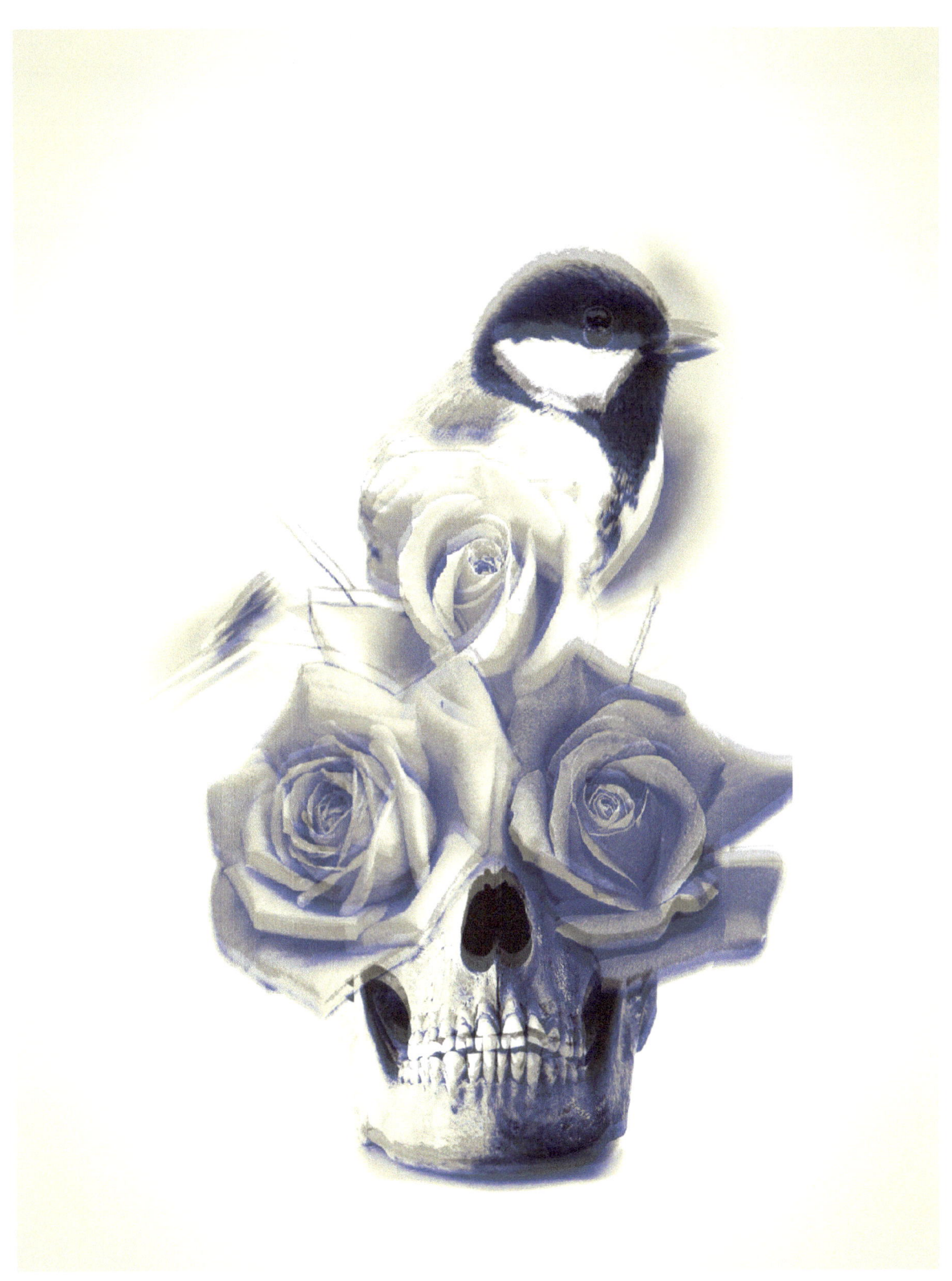

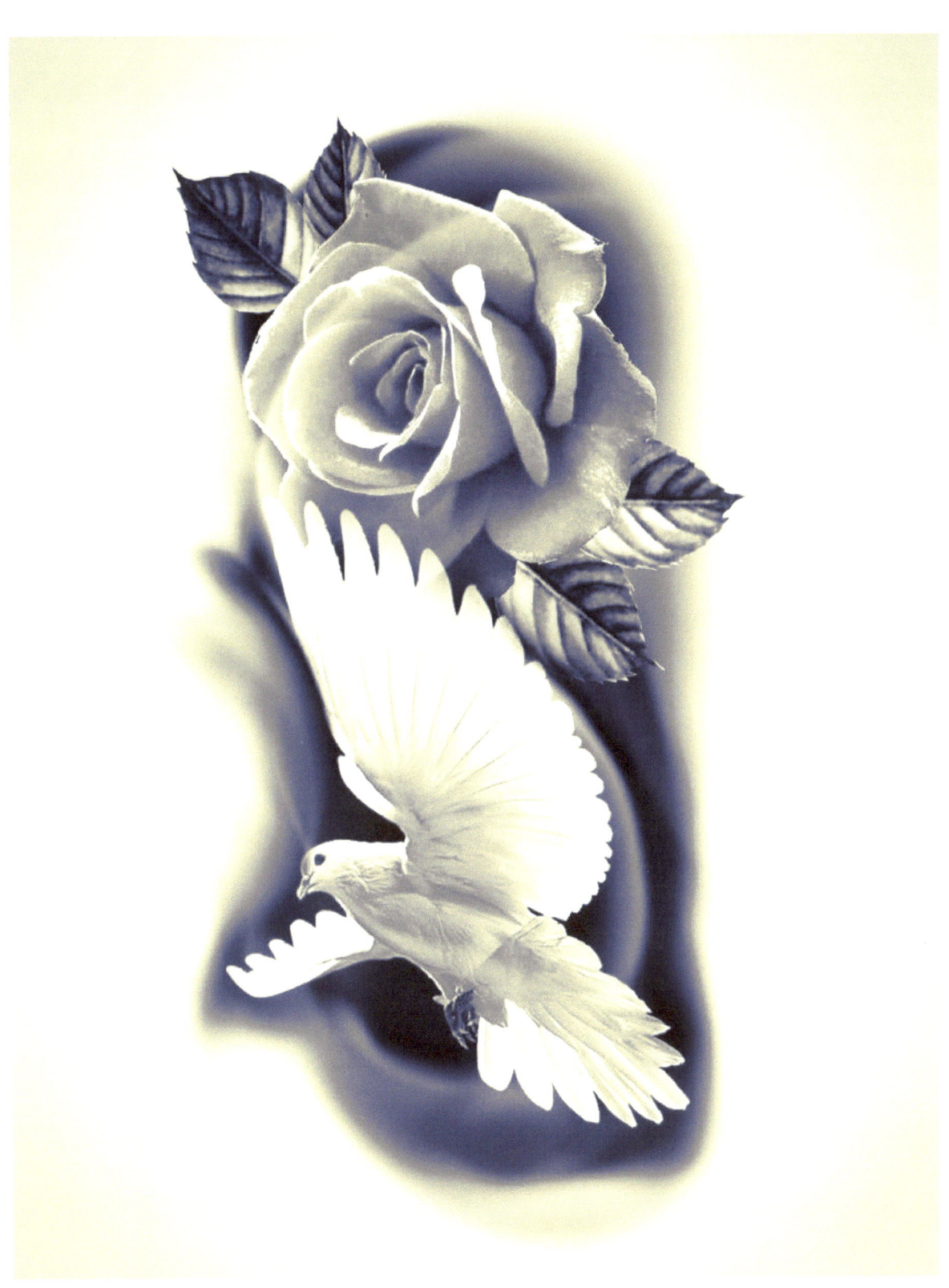

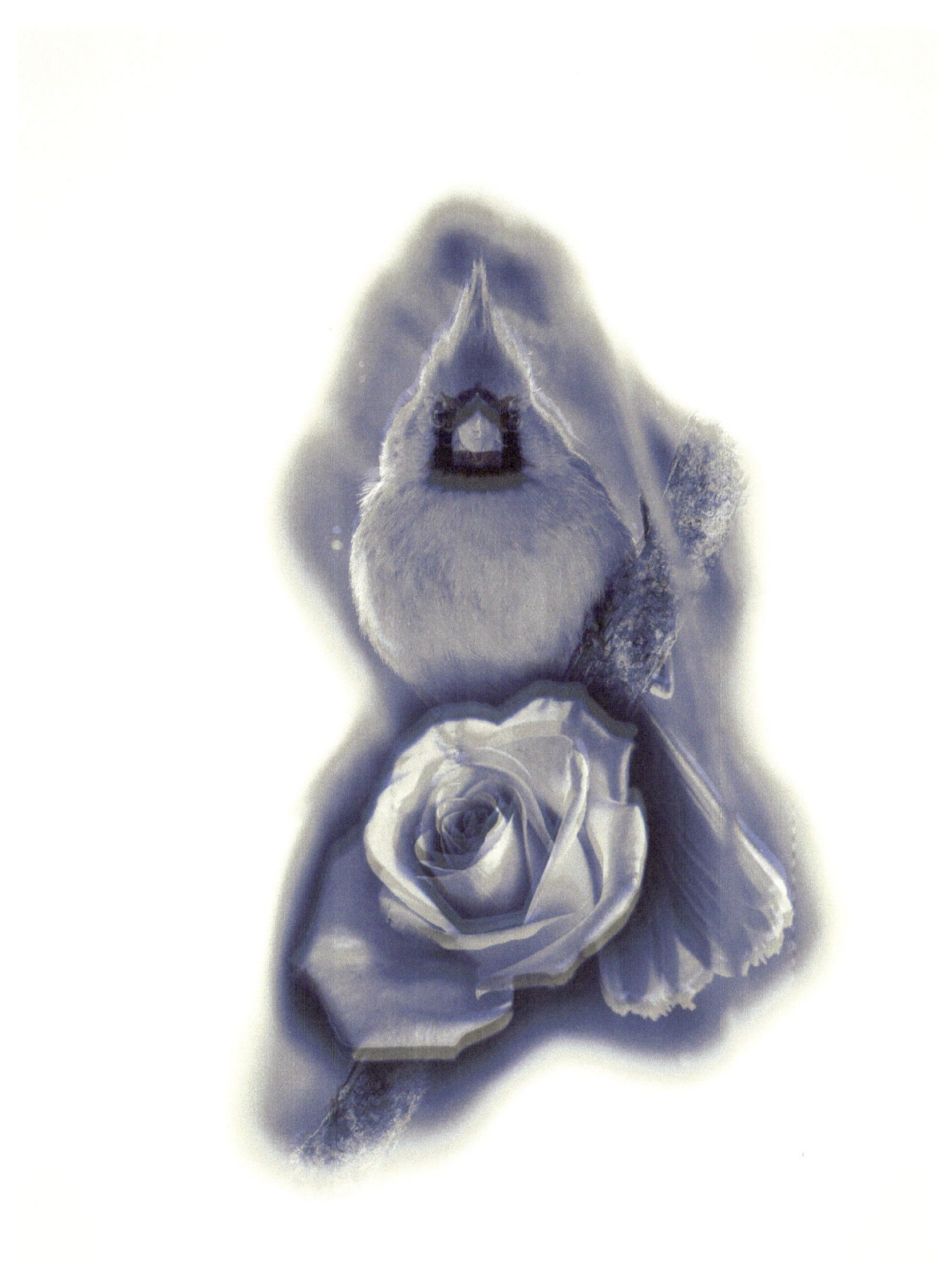

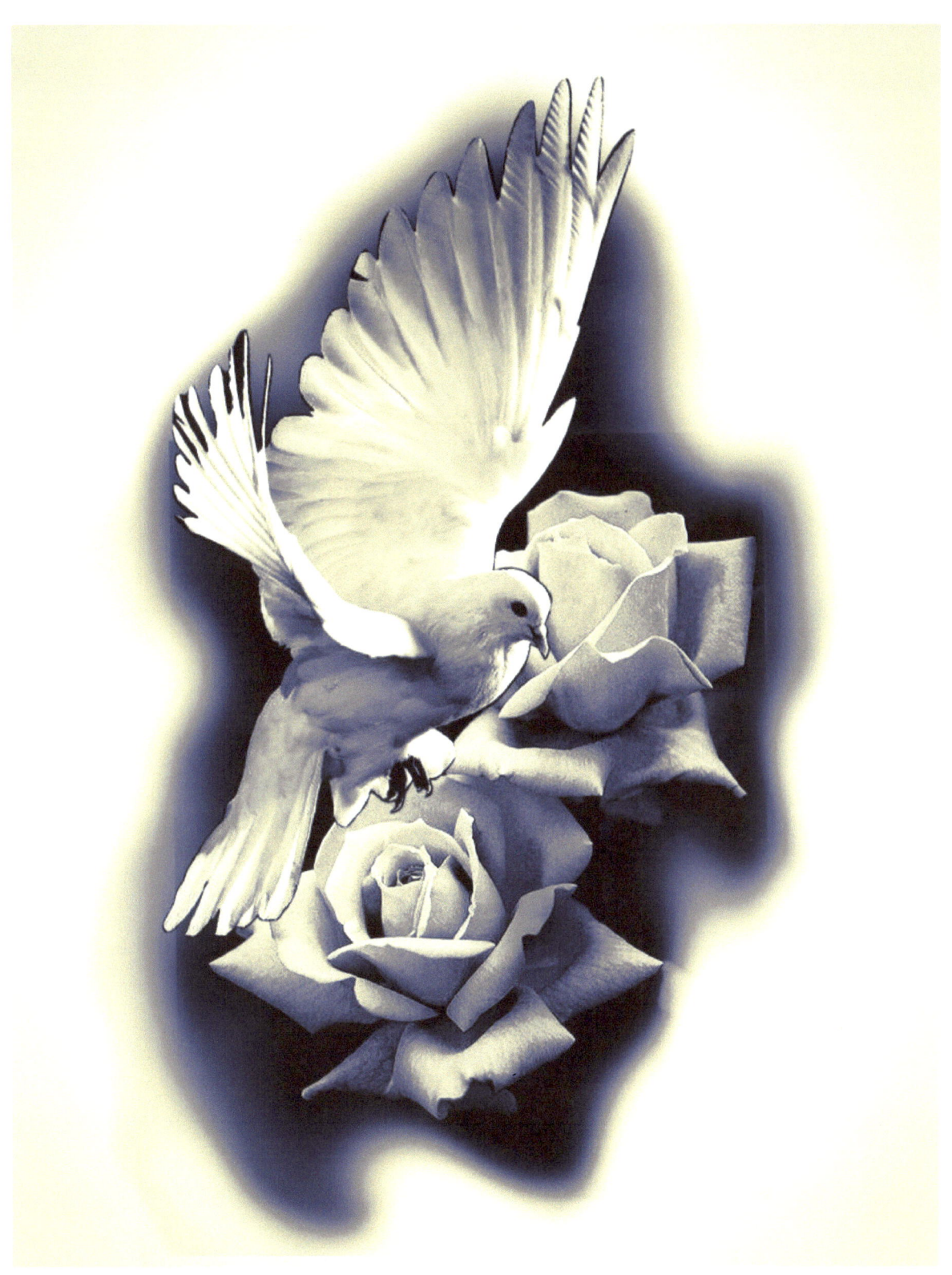

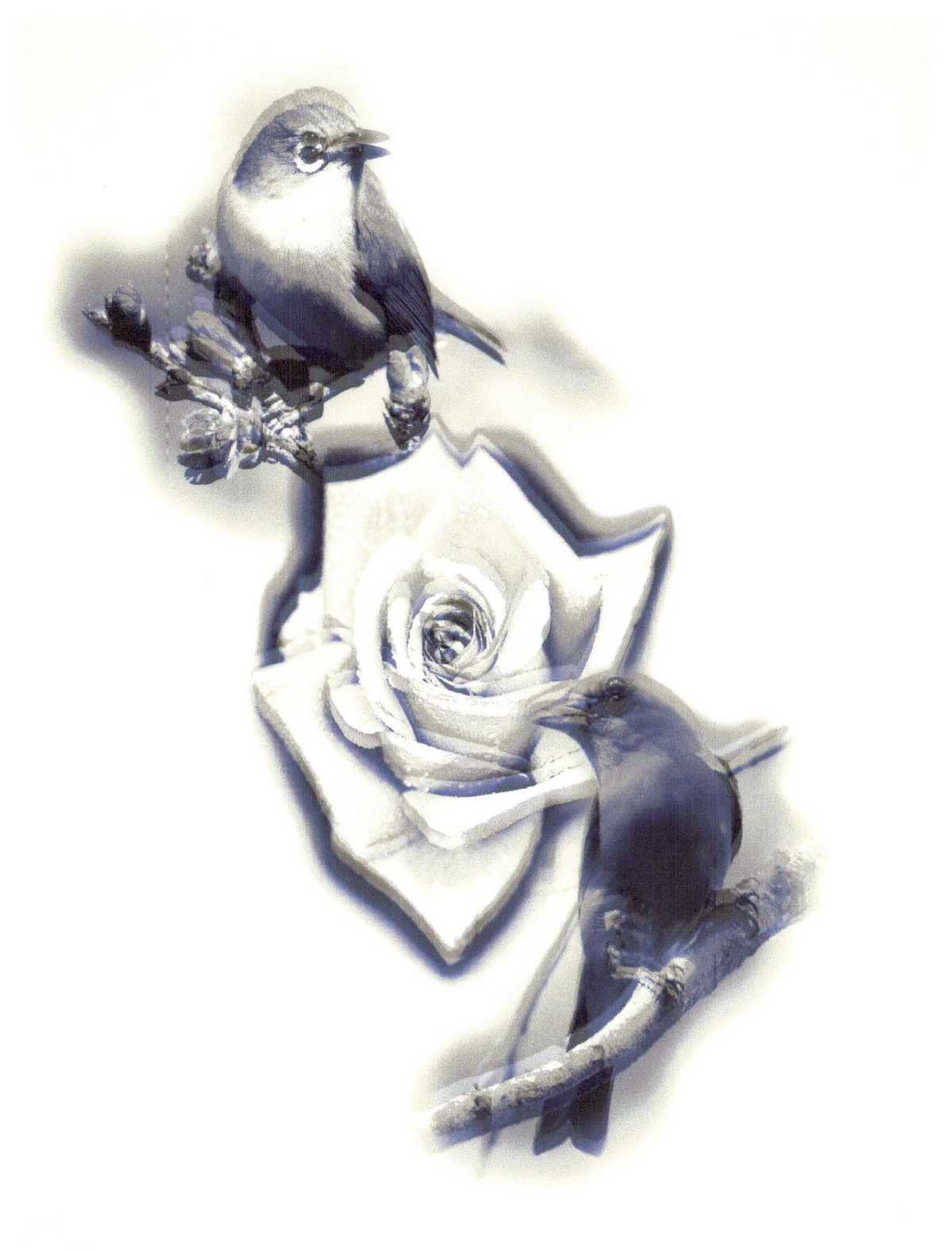

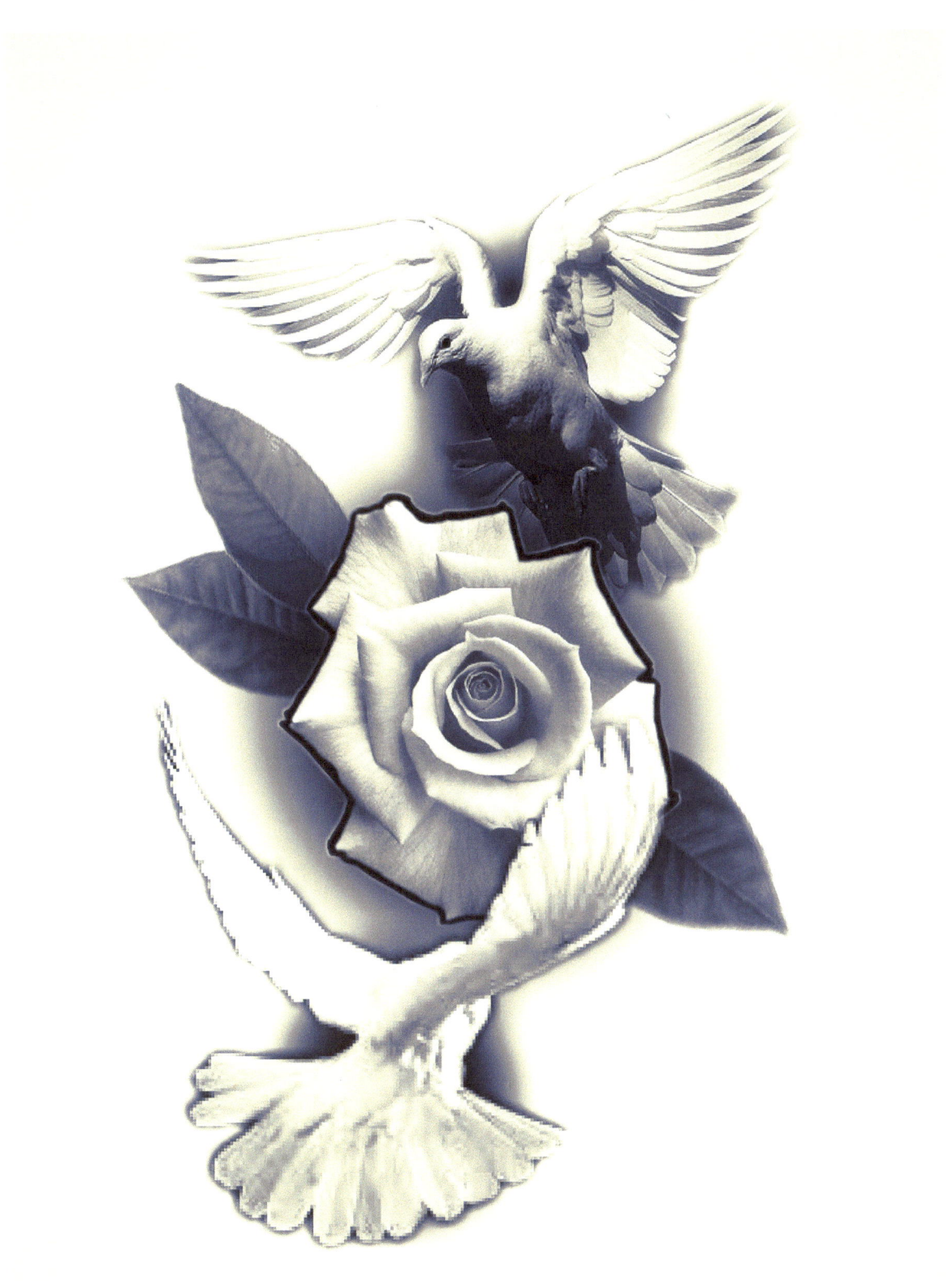

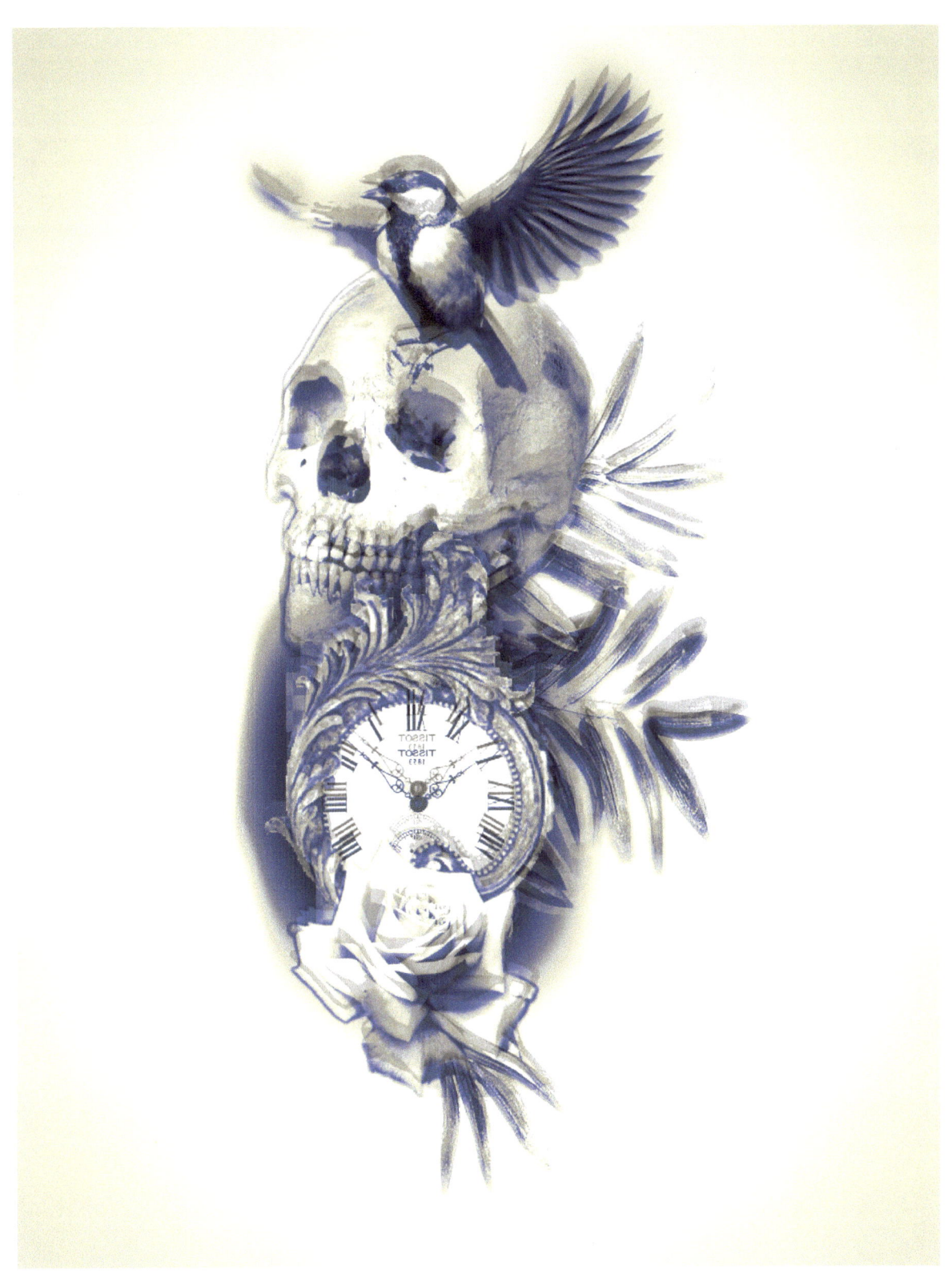

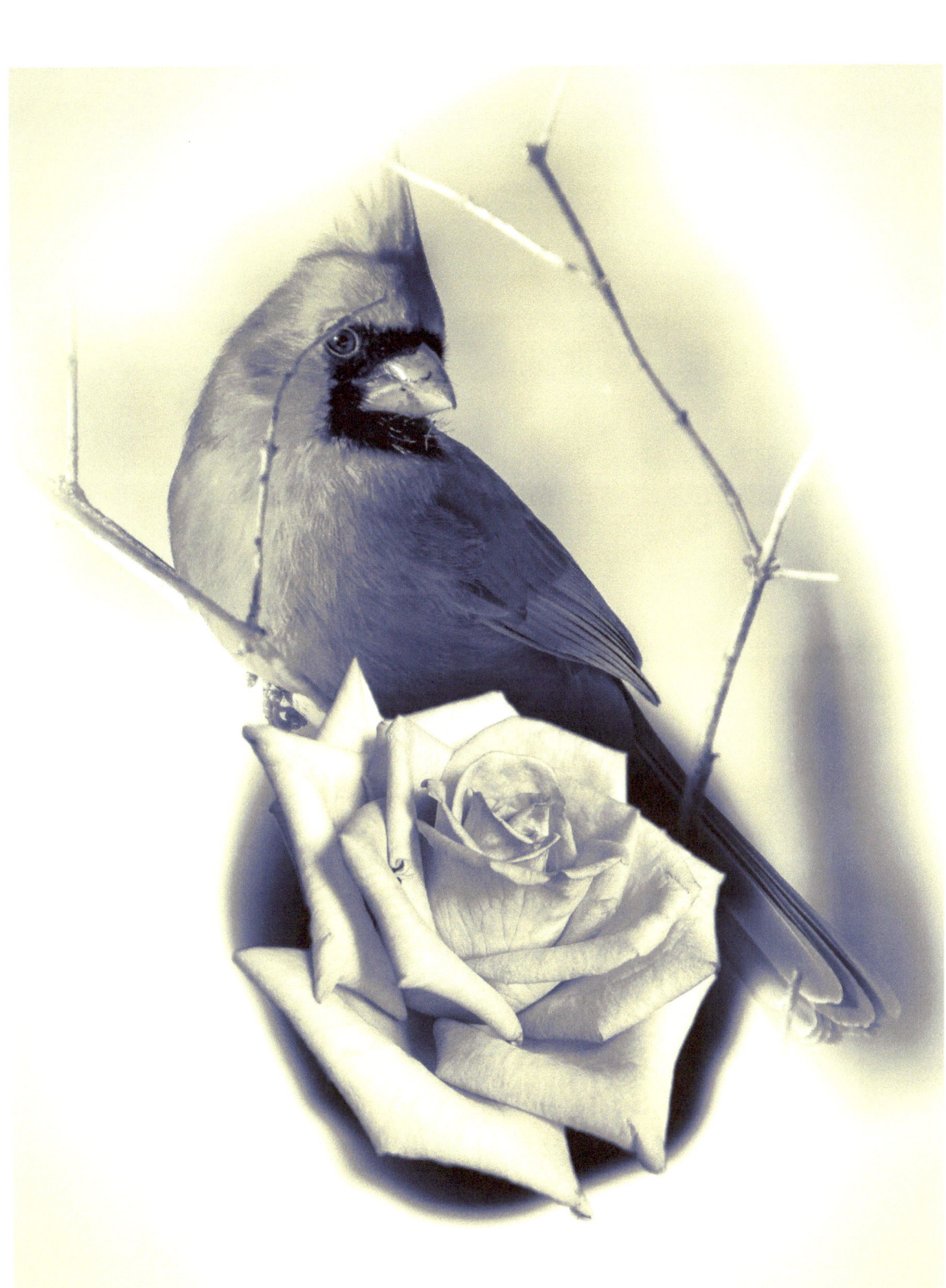

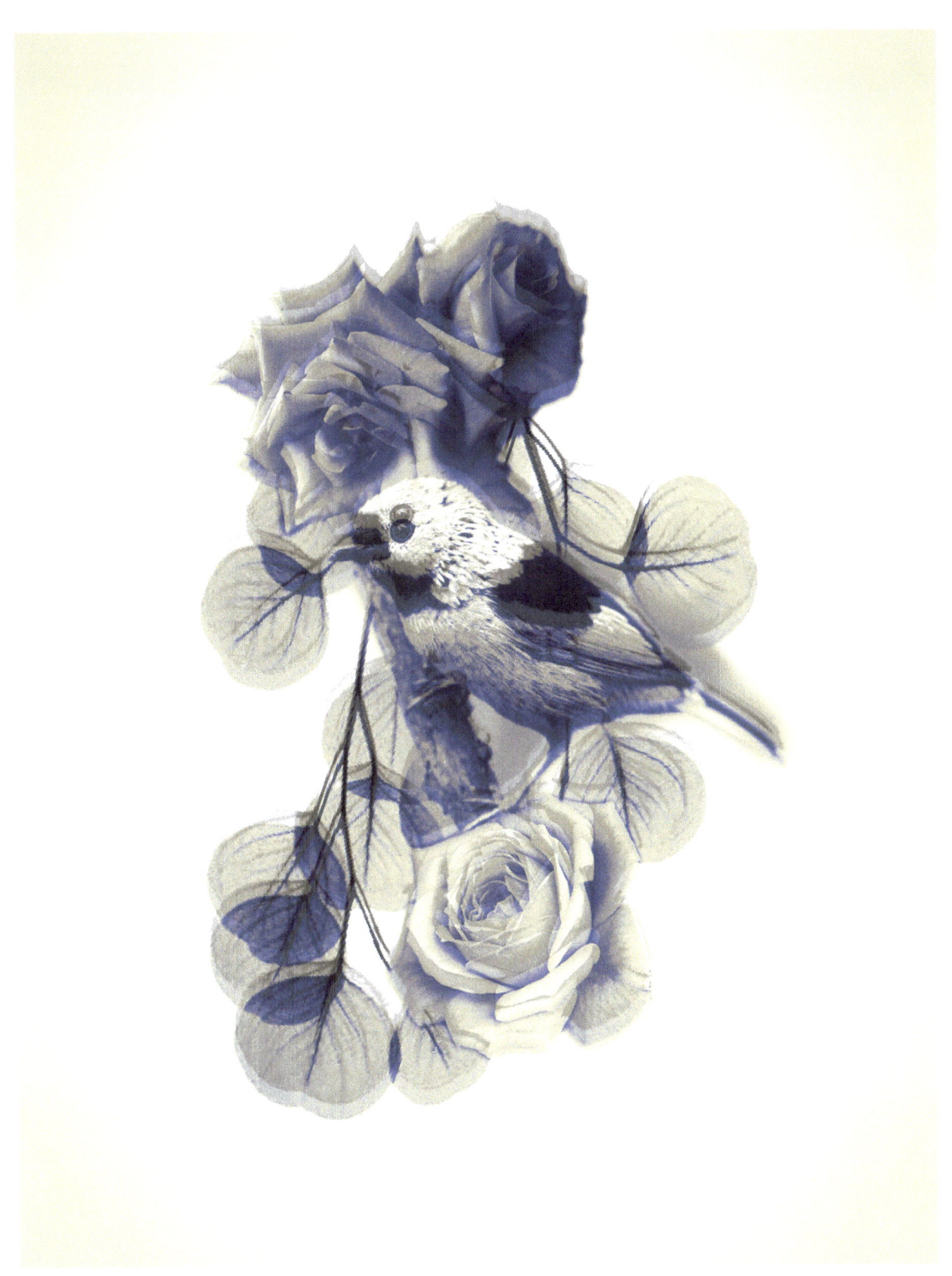

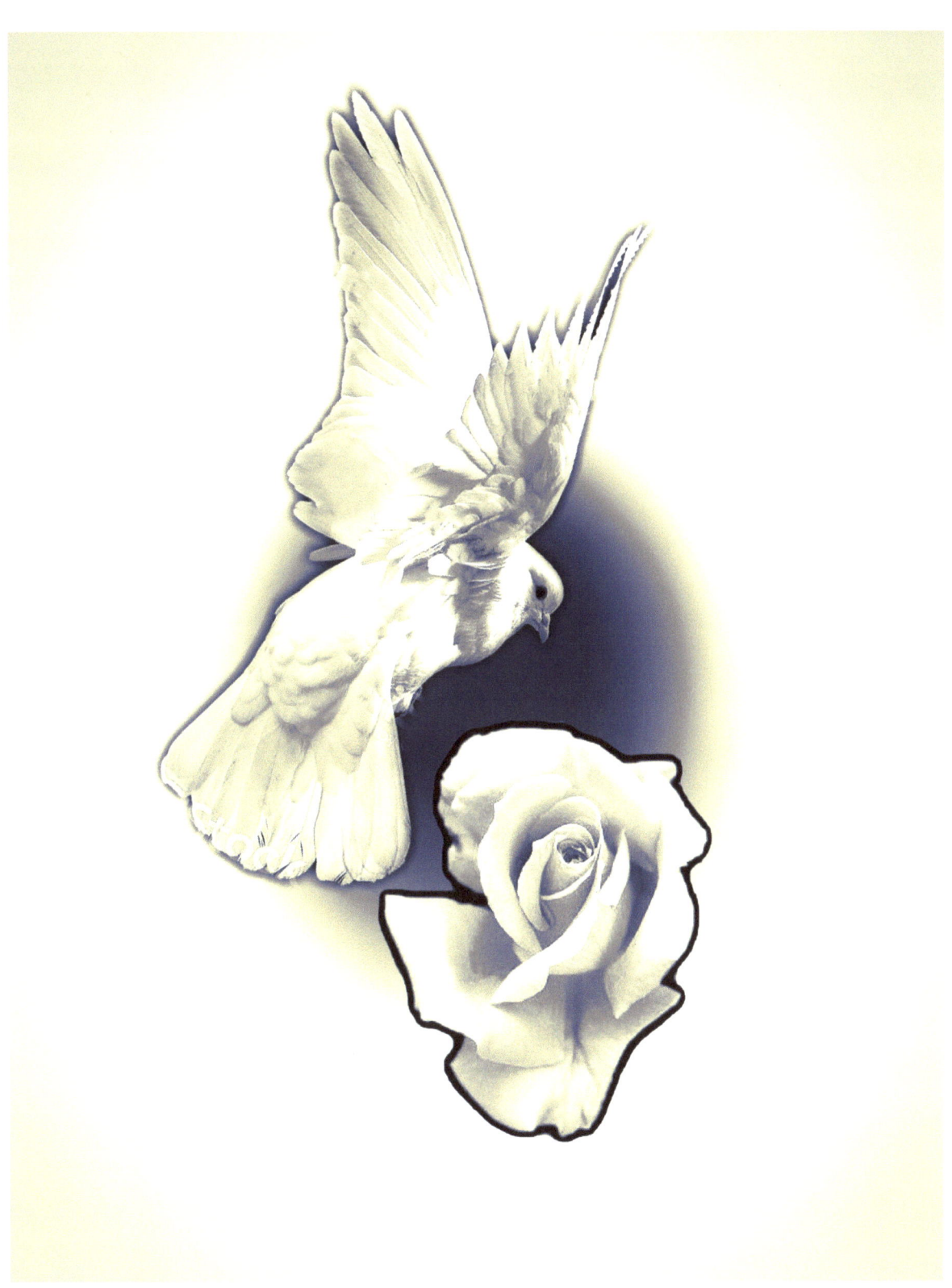

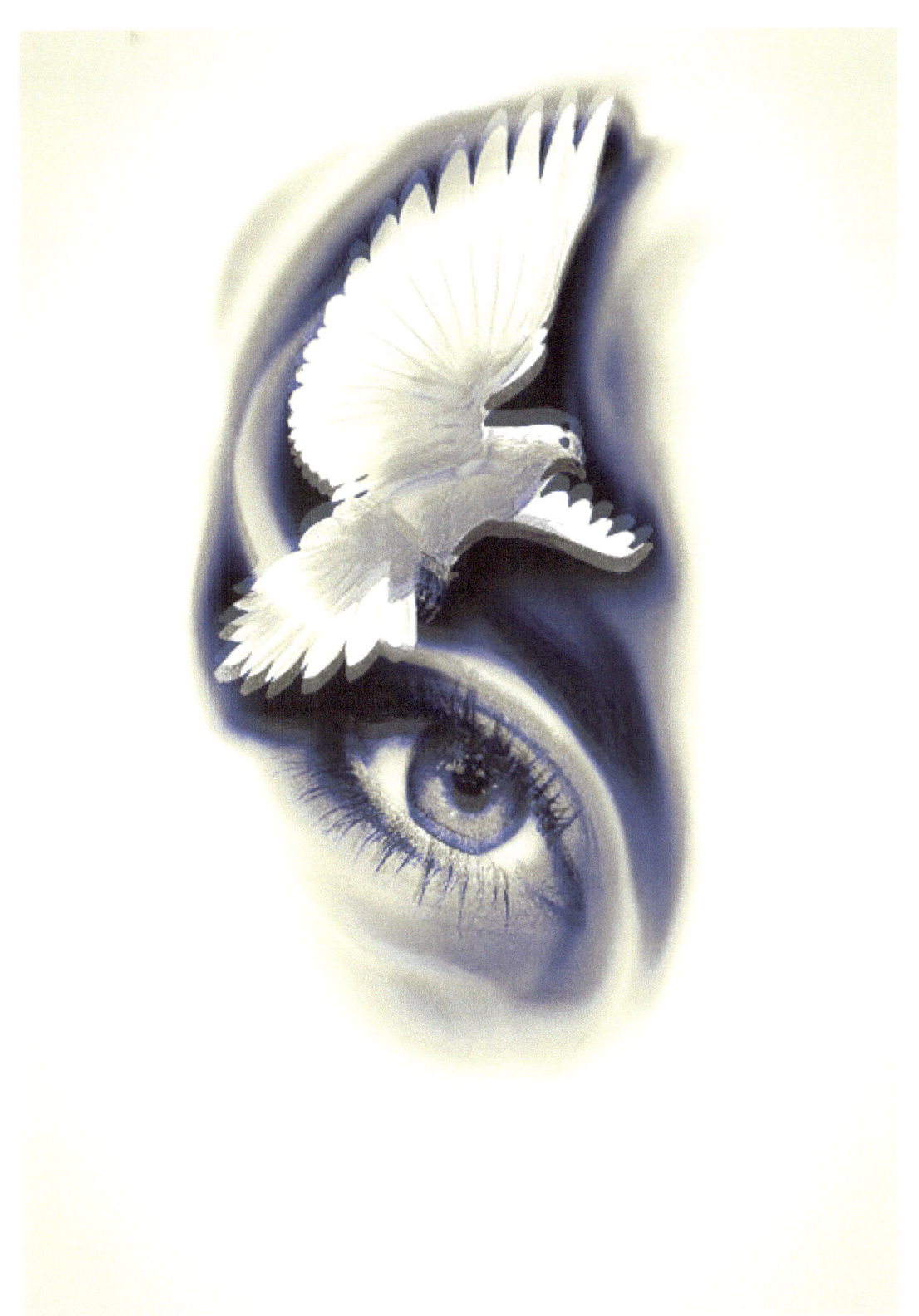

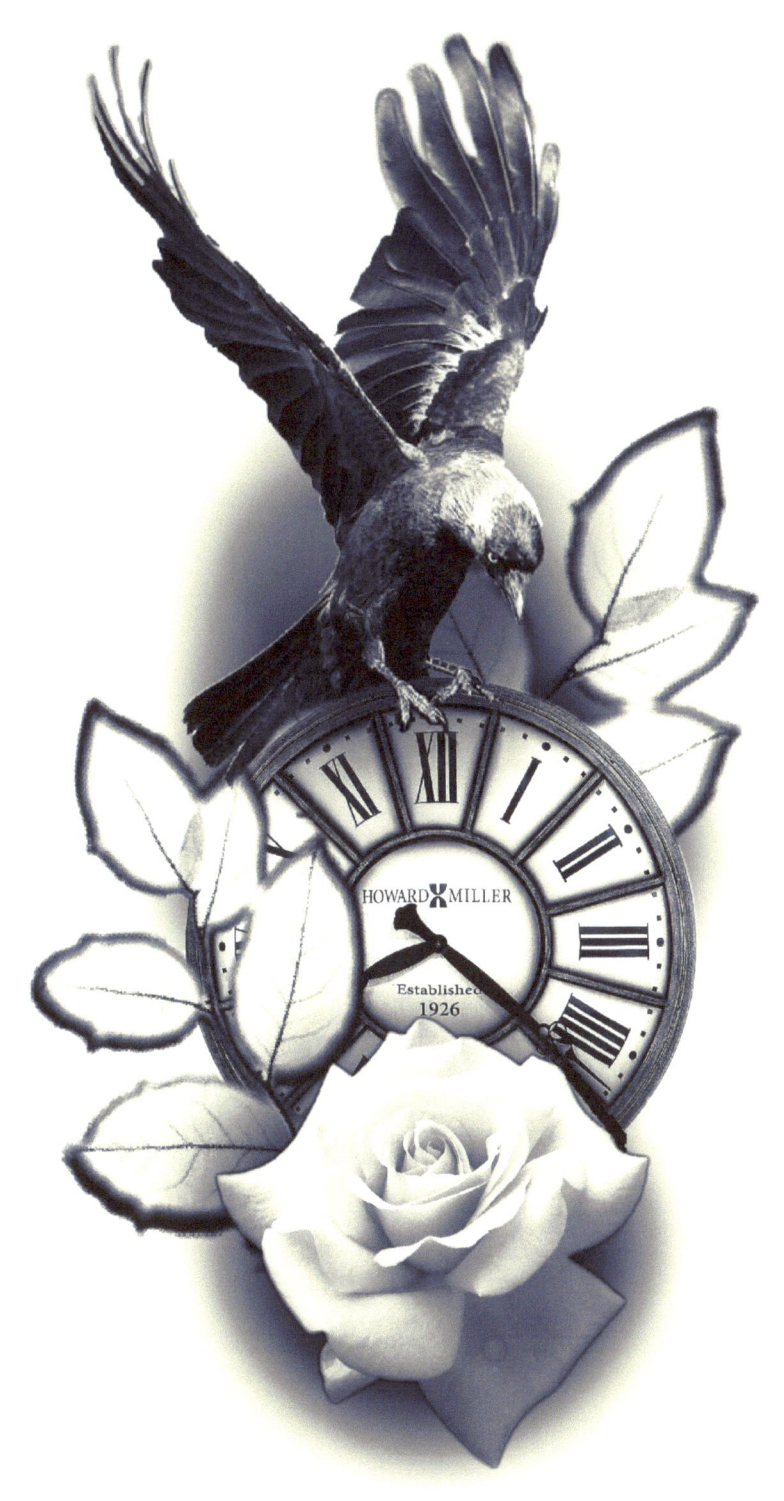

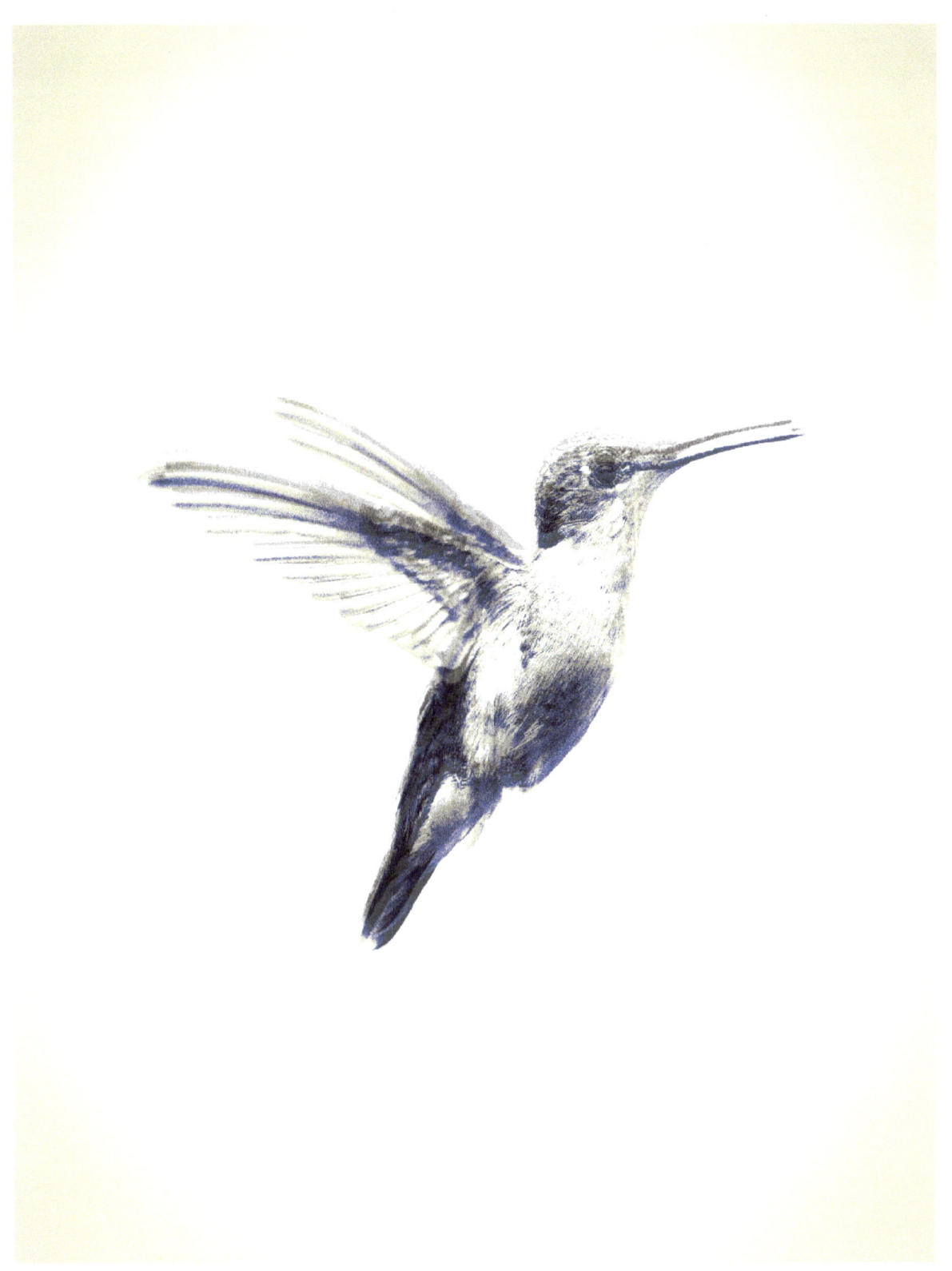

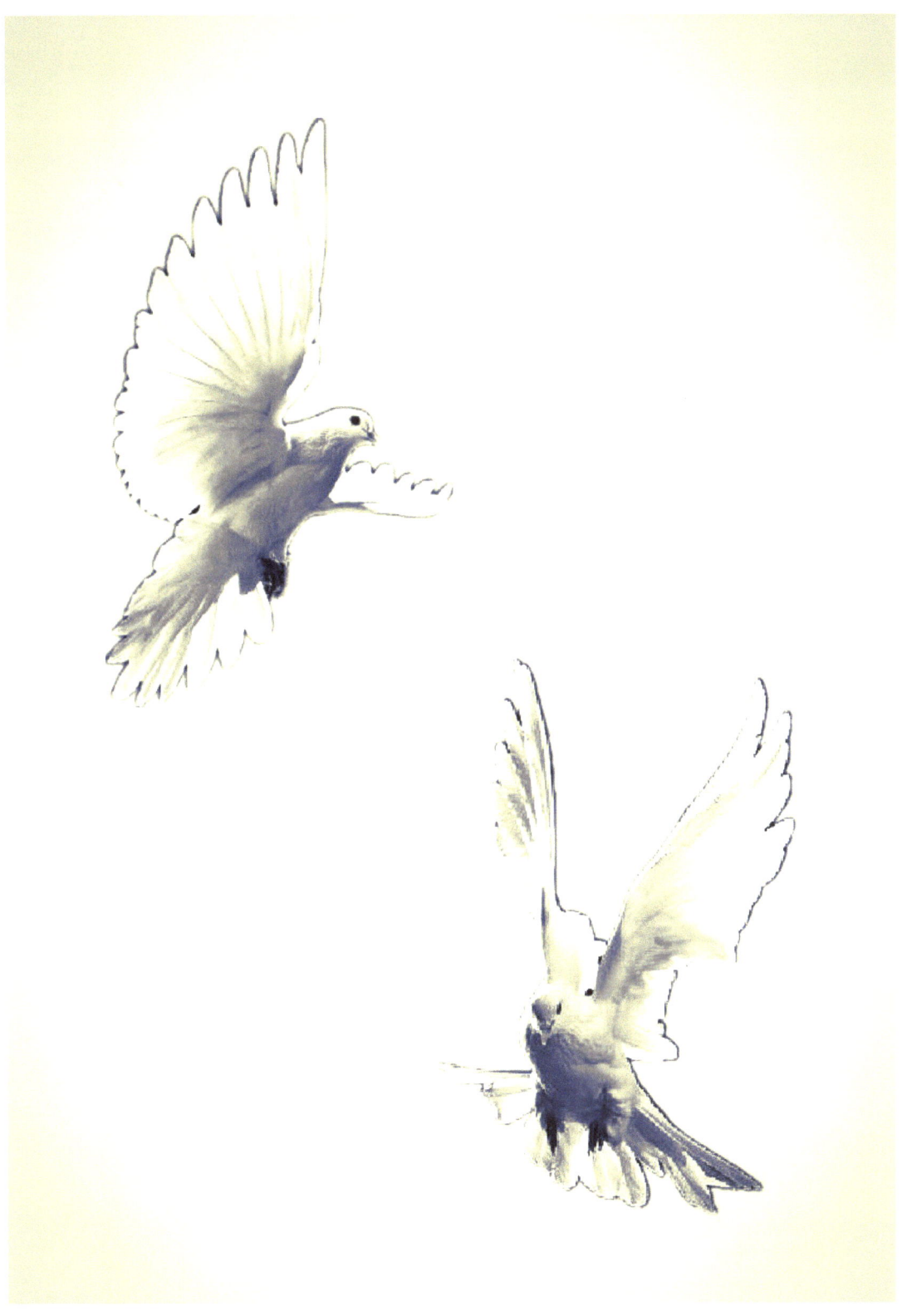

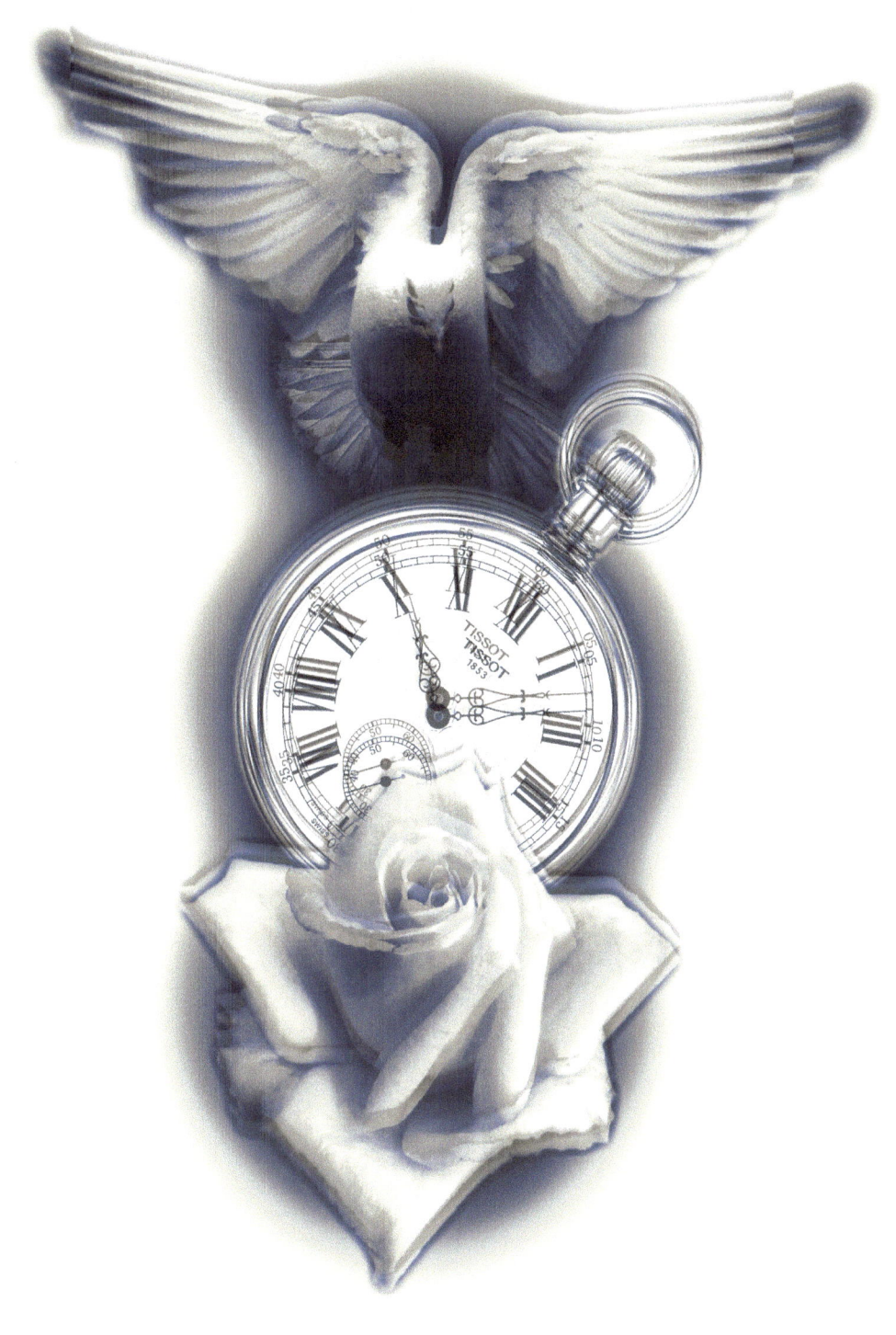

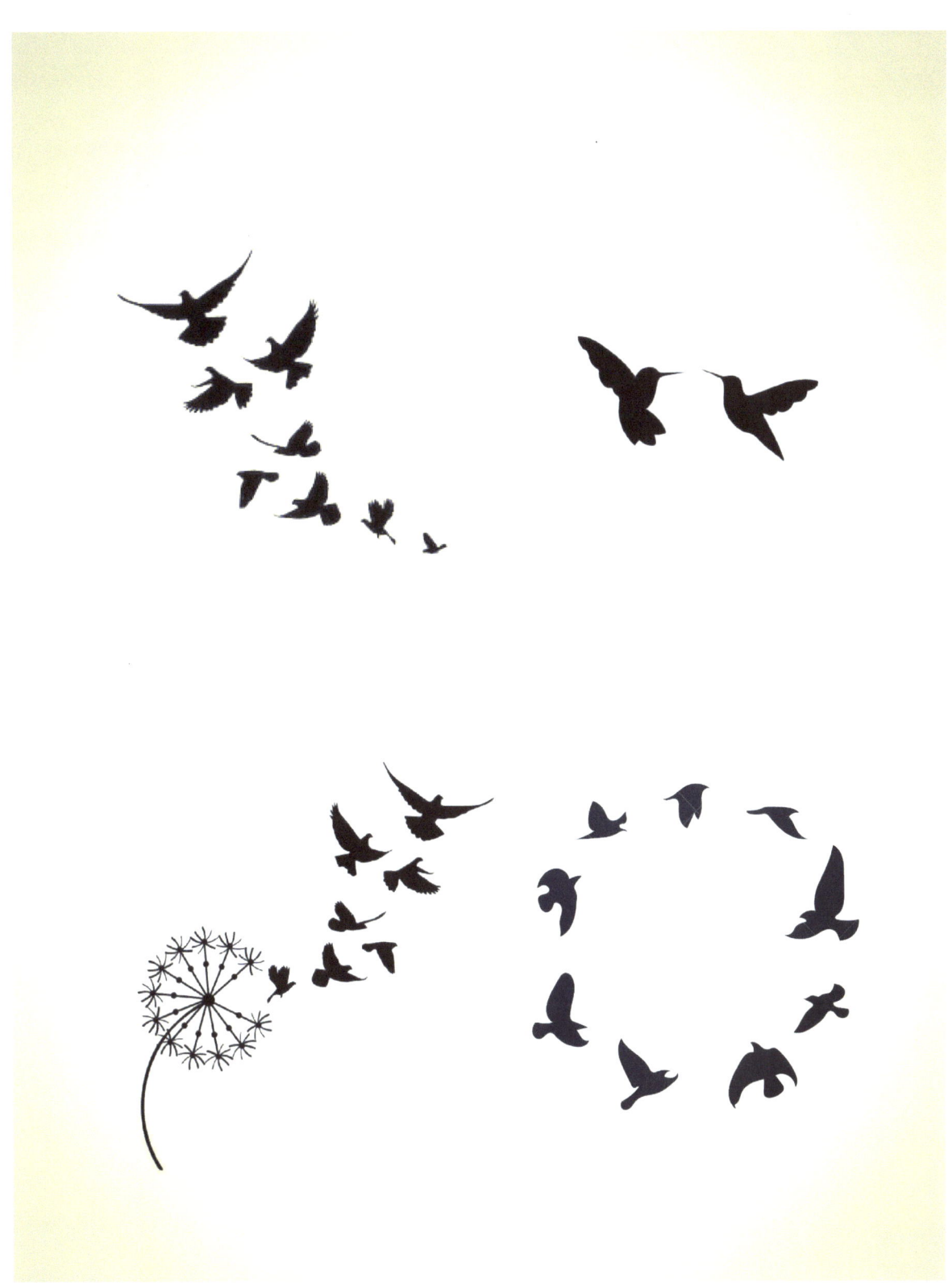

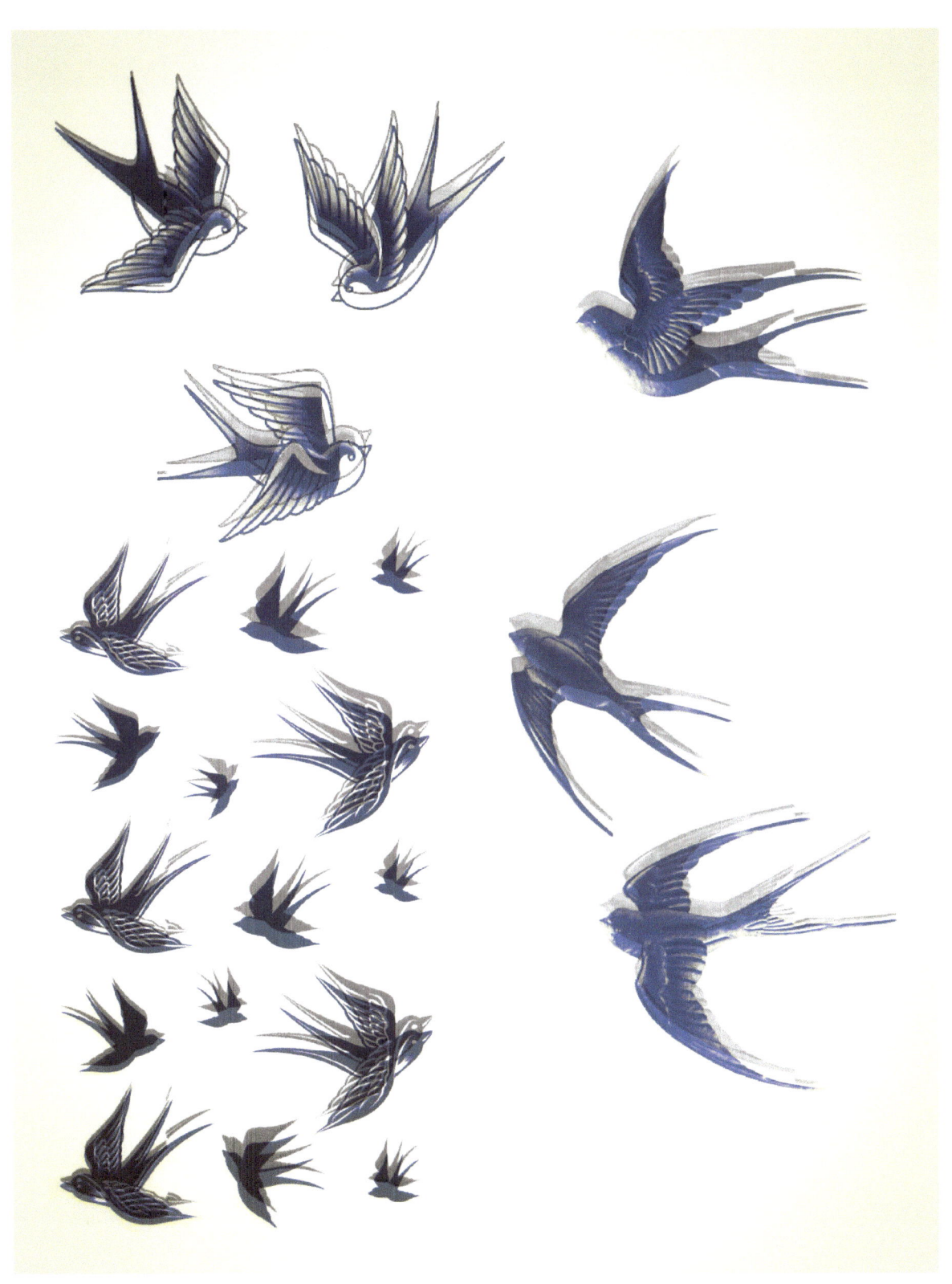

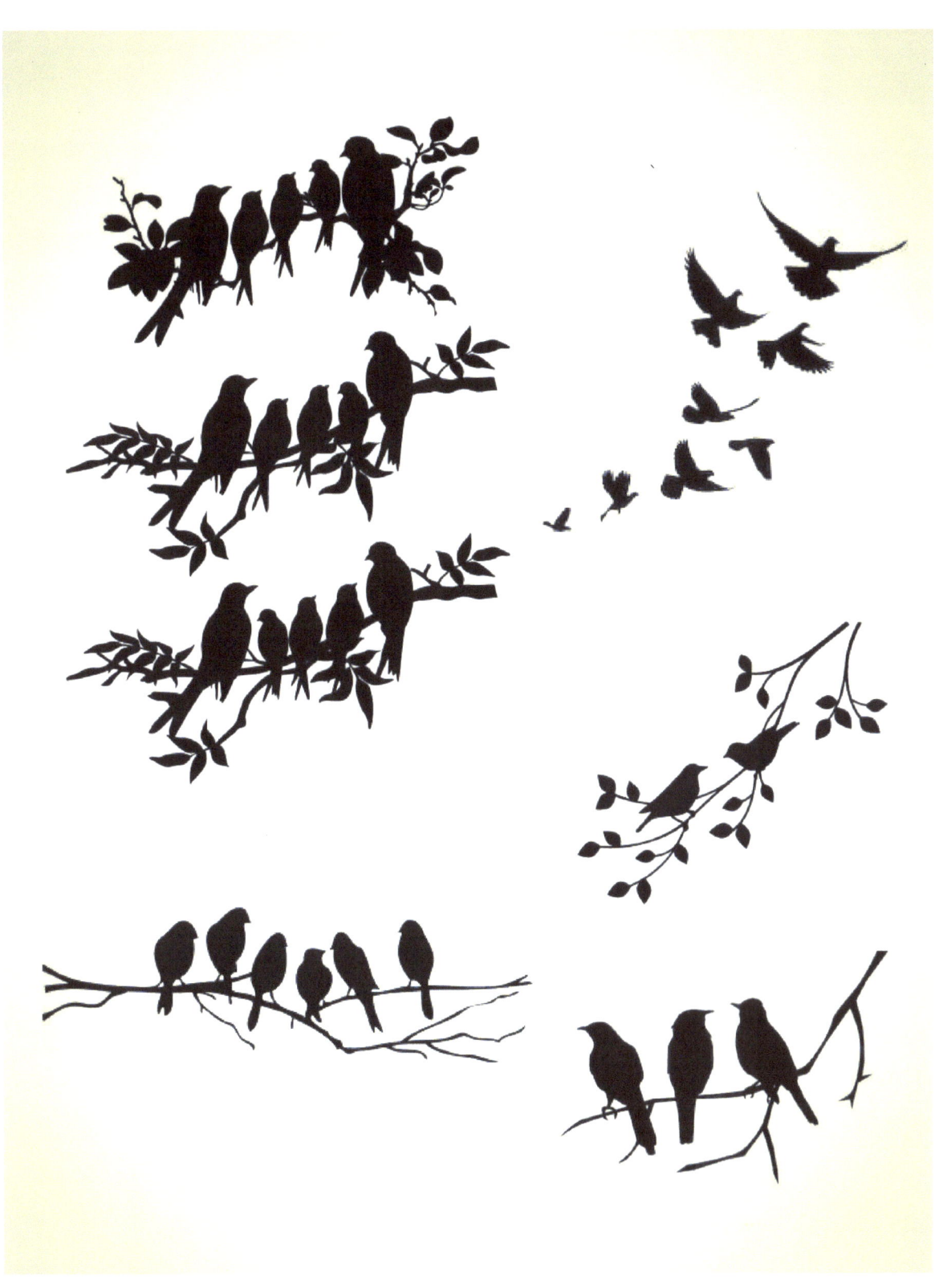

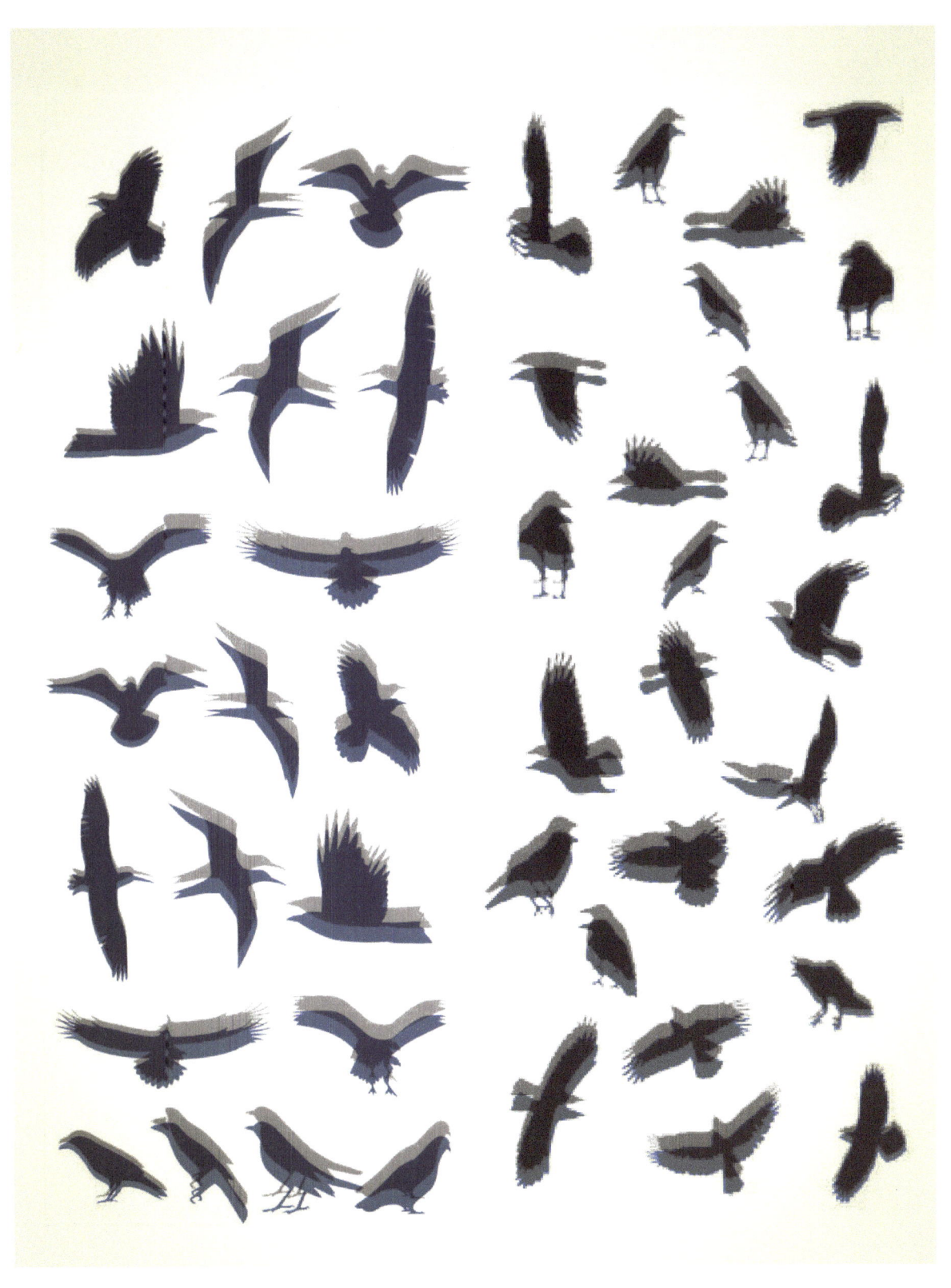

About Author

Leezey Tattoo

Pg 61 — About

www.ingramcontent.com/pod-product-compliance
Lightning Source LLC
Chambersburg PA
CBHW051920210526

45473CB00006B/2083

DIAMOND ELITE

CONTENT

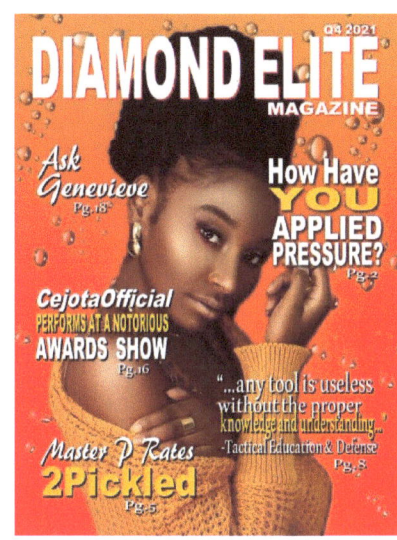

Check out the stories inside this issue!

Features

Pg.2 – ADY Program
Pg.4 – Norma's Bath & Body
Pg.8 – Tactical Education & Defense
Pg.12 – Peace Comes with Rain

Pg.14 – Fall Recipes
Pg.16 – CejotaOfficial
Pg.18 – Ask Genevieve
Pg.20 – 7 Side Ideas to Begin
Pg.22 – Good News
Pg.24 – Advertise with Us!

DIAMOND ELITE
Magazine & Co.

Diamond Elite Magazine's goal is to boost the exposure and sales of entrepreneurs.

We believe networking, circulation and word of mouth are the biggest essentials when it comes to small business.

As the years continue, we plan to thrive in success and help expand the small businesses who have contributed along the way

Be sure to take a photo of an ad inside and contact the small business owners/entrepreneurs directly if you would like to purchase a product or service!

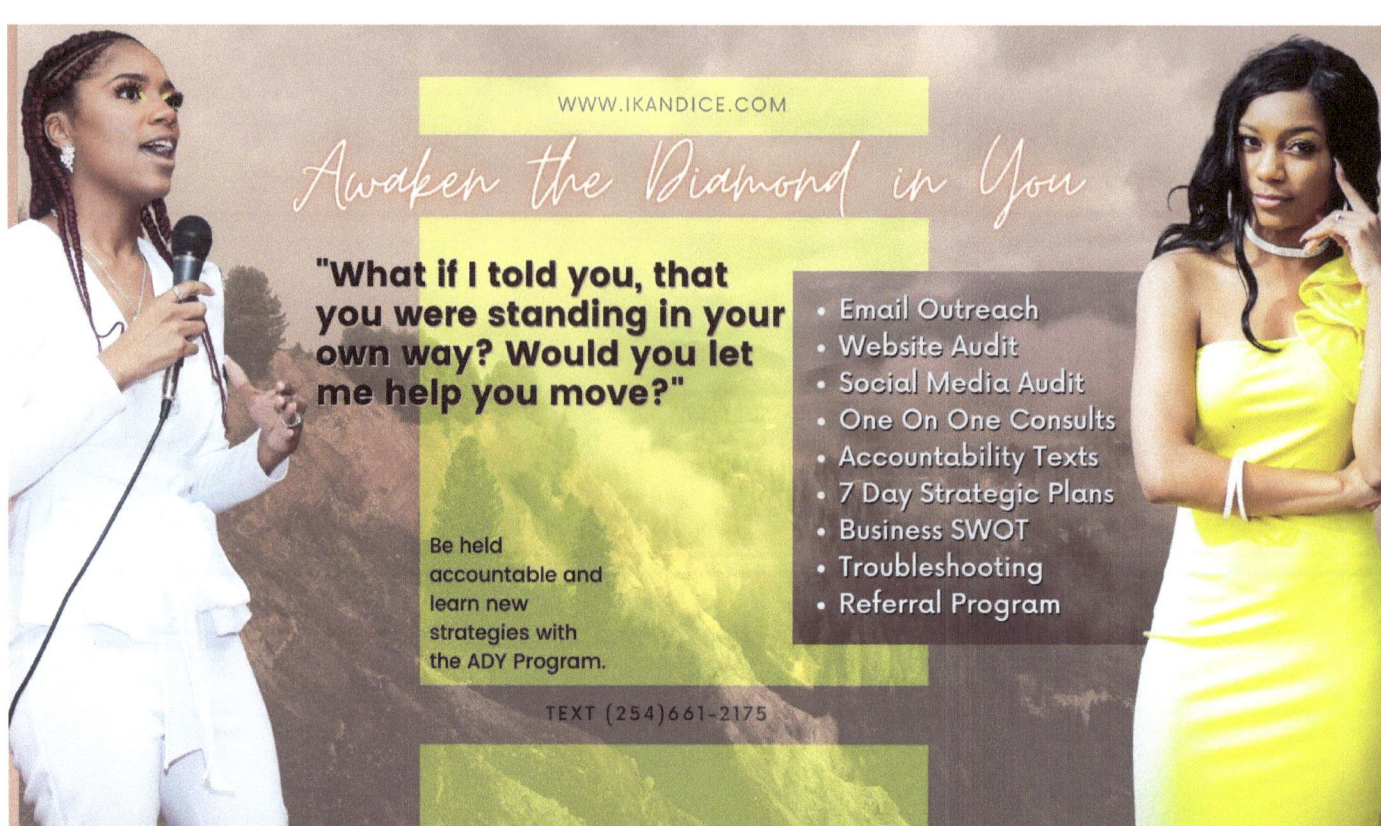

Kandice Sherril holds a degree in Business Foundations, and certifications in Leadership Development. None other than that she has over a decade in experience within the entrepreneur world.

Her mission is to assist as many entrepreneurs as she can on their journey. Kandice believes that entrepreneurs could go further in the beginning if they had more guidance and knowledge in the field of properly structuring their business, knowing about the upcoming battles beforehand, and accountability.

This is the reason for the creation of the *Awaken the Diamond in You* program, which consists of: Email Outreach, Website/Social Media Audit, Consults, Accountability Tests, Strategic Plans, Troubleshooting, and even a Referral Program that can make you money back!

Testimonials:

"I am super satisfied. You are a natural at what you do that's why you're so great, and you top it with exceptional customer service…"

- T. Brown

"Thank you so much! You're very professional. You DIDN'T make me feel bad for asking you a million questions…"

- A. Thomas

"Honest, dependable and knowledgeable, and a pleasure to work with…"

- S. Smith